States

NEW HAMPSHIRE

by Jordan Mills

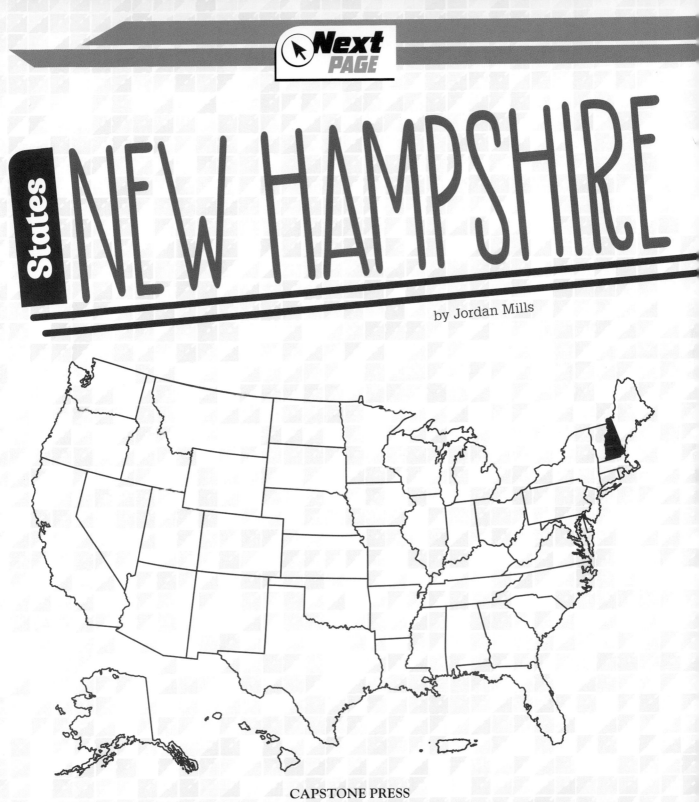

CAPSTONE PRESS
a capstone imprint

Next Page Books are published by Capstone Press,
1710 Roe Crest Drive, North Mankato, Minnesota 56003
www.mycapstone.com

Library of Congress Cataloging-in-Publication Data
Cataloging-in-publication information is on file with the Library of
Congress.
ISBN 978-1-5157-0416-4 (library binding)
ISBN 978-1-5157-0475-1 (paperback)
ISBN 978-1-5157-0527-7 (ebook PDF)

Editorial Credits
Jaclyn Jaycox, editor; Richard Korab and Katy LaVigne, designers;
Morgan Walters, media researcher; Tori Abraham, production specialist

Photo Credits
Alamy: Eric Carr, 29, North Wind Picture Archives, 25; Capstone Press:
Angie Gahler, map 4, 7; CriaImages.com: Jay Robert Nash Collection,
top 18, middle 18, top 19, middle 19; Getty Images: Getty Images
Entertainment/Jonathan Fickles, bottom 19; Glow Images: Tom Till,
11; iStockphoto: DenisTangneyJr, 5; Library of Congress: Civil War
photographs, 1861–1865/compiled by Hirst D. Milhollen and Donald
H. Mugridge, Washington, D.C., 27, Prints and Photographs Division
Washington, D.C., 26; One Mile Up, Inc., flag, seal 23; Shutterstock: Art
Phaneuf Photography, bottom left 8, CO Leong, 16, Denis Tabler, bottom
right 20, Dmitry Kalinovsky, 15, Doug Lemke, 6, Erick Margarita
Images, middle left 21, Everett Historical, 12, Hugo Felix, 14, Igor
Sinkov, top 24, Jeff Feverston, top left 21, Jo Ann Snover, cover, Jon
Bilous, 7, kzww, top left 20, Larsek, bottom right 21, Maryna Pleshkun,
top right 20, Olivier Le Queinec, 13, Patrick Lienin, bottom right 8,
Robert Manley, 9, Sean Donohue Photo, 10, Steve Byland, bottom left
20, Taras Garkusha, bottom 24, Tom Reichner, middle right 21, Warren
Bouton, 17; U.S. Fish and Wildlife Serivce: Hollingsworth, J & K,
bottom left 21; Wikimedia: NASA Human Space Flight Gallery, bottom
18, 28, Steven G. Johnson, top right 21

All design elements by Shutterstock

Printed and bound in China.
0316/CA21600187
012016   009436F16

TABLE OF CONTENTS

Want to take your research further? Ask your librarian if your school subscribes to PebbleGo Next. If so, when you see this helpful symbol ⒦ throughout the book, log onto www.pebblegonext.com for bonus downloads and information.

LOCATION

New Hampshire is one of the New England states. It's located in the nation's northeast corner. Just north of New Hampshire is Canada. To the west is Vermont. Massachusetts is to the south. Maine is to the east. Southeastern New Hampshire borders the Atlantic Ocean. The capital city of Concord lies along the Merrimack River, which runs through the center of the state. Manchester, Nashua, Concord, Dover, and Rochester are the state's largest cities.

PebbleGo Next Bonus!
To print and label your own map, go to www.pebblegonext.com and search keywords:

NH MAP

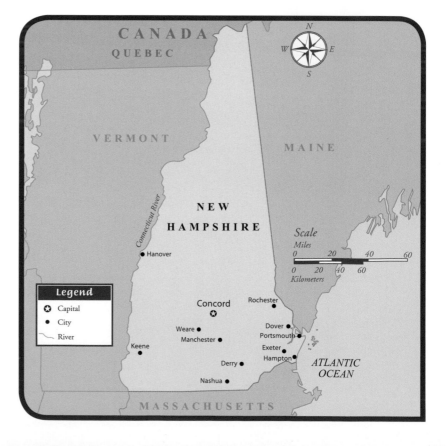

Located on the banks of the Merrimack River, Manchester is New Hampshire's largest city.

GEOGRAPHY

Mountains, farmland, seashore, and lakes are all part of New Hampshire's geography. The White Mountains stretch from central New Hampshire into western Maine. The Presidential Range has the highest peaks in New England. Mount Washington is the highest of these peaks. This mountain is 6,288 feet (1,917 meters) high. South of the White Mountains are the Lakes Region, the Merrimack River Valley, and the Coastal Lowlands. New Hampshire has 13 miles (21 kilometers) of coastline along the Atlantic Ocean.

PebbleGo Next Bonus!
To watch a video about Cog Railway, go to www.pebblegonext.com and search keywords:
NH VIDEO

New Hampshire has the least amount of shoreline of any ocean-bordering state.

The peaks in the Presidential Range of the White Mountains are all named after U.S. presidents.

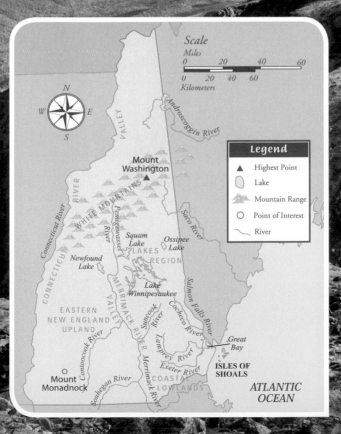

Scale

Miles
0   20   40   60

0   20   40   60
Kilometers

N
W   E
S

Androscoggin River

VALLEY

CONNECTICUT RIVER VALLEY

Connecticut River

Mount Washington ▲

WHITE MOUNTAINS

Pemigewasset River

Saco River

Squam Lake

Ossipee Lake

LAKES REGION

Newfound Lake

Lake Winnipesaukee

Salmon Falls River

CONNECTICUT

MERRIMACK VALLEY

Suncook River

Cocheco River

EASTERN NEW ENGLAND UPLAND

Contoocook River

Lamprey River

MERRIMACK RIVER

Great Bay

ISLES OF SHOALS

O Mount Monadnock

Souhegan River

Exeter River

Merrimack River

COASTAL LOWLANDS

ATLANTIC OCEAN

Legend

▲ Highest Point

⬠ Lake

⛰ Mountain Range

O Point of Interest

〰 River

WEATHER

New Hampshire summers are usually cool. The state's average annual summer temperature is 65 degrees Fahrenheit (18 degrees Celsius). New Hampshire winters are cold. The average winter temperature is 20°F (-7°C).

Average High and Low Temperatures (Concord, NH)

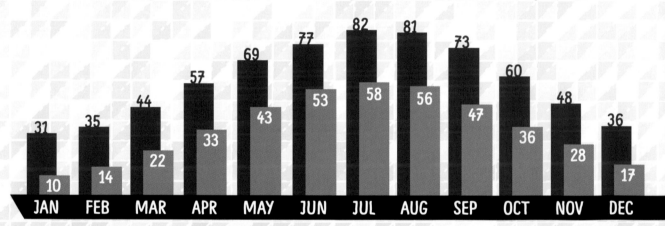

	JAN	FEB	MAR	APR	MAY	JUN	JUL	AUG	SEP	OCT	NOV	DEC
High	31	35	44	57	69	77	82	81	73	60	48	36
Low	10	14	22	33	43	53	58	56	47	36	28	17

LANDMARKS

Lake Winnipesaukee

This lake is the state's largest body of water. It is at the southern end of the White Mountains. The lake is a popular spot for boating and swimming.

Hampton Beach

This beach runs along the Atlantic coast. The Seacoast Science Center is in Rye. It provides information on the seacoast's creatures and land features to visitors.

America's Stonehenge

These stone structures, named after a group of similar stone monuments in England, are in Salem, New Hampshire. Ancient people built them more than 4,000 years ago. The stones were built to work like a calendar. Certain points line up perfectly with the sun at the change of seasons.

HISTORY AND GOVERNMENT

Captain John Smith, an English soldier, explored the east coast of North America.

Native people lived near the New Hampshire coast at least 5,000 years before European explorers arrived. By the early 1600s, the Pennacook Confederacy and the Abenaki Confederacy were the two main groups living in what is now New Hampshire. In 1603 English Captain Martin Pring sailed along the coast and up the Piscataqua River. In 1614 Captain John Smith mapped the coastline for England. New Hampshire became a royal province in 1679. New Hampshire soldiers fought for the colonies during the Revolutionary War. In 1783 the colonies defeated Great Britain. In 1788 New Hampshire became the 9th U.S. state.

New Hampshire's state government has three branches. The governor leads the executive branch, which enforces the laws. The lawmaking legislature includes the 400-member House of Representatives and the 24-member Senate. Judges and courts are the judicial branch. They uphold the laws.

New Hampshire's capitol building is the oldest in the country where legislature still meets in the original chambers.

INDUSTRY

Since the 1800s manufacturing and tourism have been the two most important industries in New Hampshire. New Hampshire factories make a variety of products, including computer hardware and software, industrial equipment, and rubber and plastic products. Some textile products are still made in the state. New Hampshire factories have built ships and weapons for the U.S. military since the Revolutionary War.

Computer and electronic products are the top manufactured goods in New Hampshire.

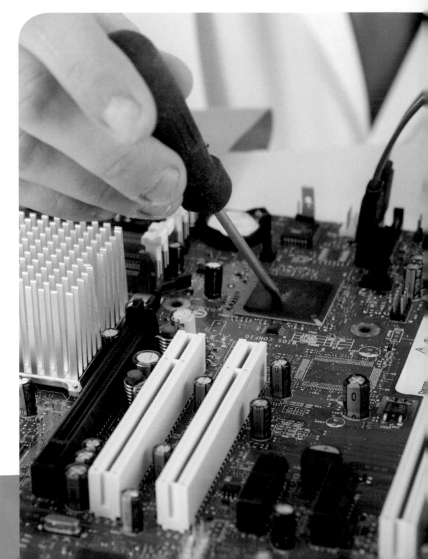

Tourists enjoy New Hampshire during all four seasons. Skiing, snowmobiling, and sledding are popular winter activities. In spring and summer, visitors golf, hike, camp, and fish. Fall brings thousands of visitors to see the colorful leaves.

New Hampshire's abundant natural resources also support agriculture, logging, and mining. New Hampshire earned its nickname, the Granite State, from its rich deposits of granite.

New Hampshire's largest granite quarry produces about 25,000 tons (22,700 metric tons) of granite each year.

POPULATION

In the 1800s and early 1900s, French-Canadian, English, Irish, and Finnish immigrants settled in New Hampshire. Descendants of these immigrants and other white residents make up about 93 percent of New Hampshire's population. There are about 1.2 million white people living in the state. At one time, many American Indians lived in New Hampshire. Today American Indians are less than 1 percent of the state's population. Other ethnic groups in New Hampshire include Hispanics, Asians, and African-Americans. Less than 3 percent of the state's residents are Hispanic, while about 2 percent are Asian. African-Americans compose about 1 percent of New Hampshire's population.

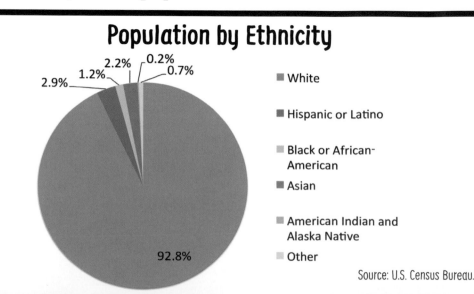

Population by Ethnicity

2.9% 1.2% 2.2% 0.2% 0.7%

92.8%

- White
- Hispanic or Latino
- Black or African-American
- Asian
- American Indian and Alaska Native
- Other

Source: U.S. Census Bureau.

FAMOUS PEOPLE

Robert Frost (1874–1963) was a poet. Many of his poems tell of the beauty of New England. Born in California, Frost lived for many years in New Hampshire.

Horace Greeley (1811–1872) was a newspaper editor and social reformer. He worked to abolish slavery. Greeley founded the *New York Tribune*.

Christa McAuliffe (1948–1986) was a Concord High School social studies teacher. On the space shuttle *Challenger*, she and the other crew members died when the spacecraft exploded. She was born in Massachusetts.

Franklin Pierce (1804–1869) was the 14th U.S. president (1853–1857). He was born in Hillsborough. Pierce, a Democrat, served one term in the White House.

Daniel Webster (1782–1852) was a political leader and a powerful speaker. He was U.S. secretary of state twice (1841–1843 and 1850–1852).

Tomie dePaola (1934–) is a children's book writer and illustrator. He has published more than 200 children's books. He has won both Caldecott Honor and Newbery Honor awards. He was born in Connecticut and currently lives and works in New London, New Hampshire.

STATE SYMBOLS

Tree

white birch

Flower

purple lilac

Bird

purple finch

Insect

ladybug

PebbleGo Next Bonus! To make a sweeet treat using one of New Hampshire's major food products, go to www.pebblegonext.com and search keywords: **NH RECIPE**

Freshwater Fish

brook trout

Saltwater Game Fish

striped bass

Gemstone

smoky quartz

Animal

white-tailed deer

Butterfly

Karner blue

Amphibian

red-spotted newt

FAST FACTS

STATEHOOD
1788

CAPITAL ☆
Concord

LARGEST CITY •
Manchester

SIZE
8,953 square miles (23,188 square kilometers)
land area (2010 U.S. Census Bureau)

POPULATION
1,323,459 (2013 U.S. Census estimate)

STATE NICKNAME
Granite State

STATE MOTTO
"Live Free or Die"

STATE SEAL

The first New Hampshire state seal was created in 1775. Many changes were made over the years. The legislature created a permanent seal in 1931. The words "Seal of the State of New Hampshire, 1776" wrap around the circle. The warship *Raleigh* is in the center of the seal. Built in 1776, the *Raleigh* was one of the first Navy warships. A wreath of laurel leaves surrounds the *Raleigh*. A granite boulder near the ship stands for the state's rocky land.

PebbleGo Next Bonus!
To print and color your own flag, go to www.pebblegonext.com and search keywords:
NH FLAG ⟳

STATE FLAG

New Hampshire adopted its state flag in 1909. The flag was changed slightly in 1931 when the legislature adopted an official state seal. The flag is dark blue. The state seal is in the center. Laurel leaves and nine stars surround the seal. The stars represent New Hampshire's position as the 9th state.

MINING PRODUCTS

sand and gravel, gemstones, granite, traprock

MANUFACTURED GOODS

computer and electronic equipment, fabricated metal products, machinery, food products, plastics and rubber products, electrical equipment, nonmetallic mineral products, chemicals

FARM PRODUCTS

dairy products, greenhouse products, maple syrup, hay, feed corn, apples, vegetables

PebbleGo Next Bonus! To learn the lyrics to the state song, go to www.pebblegonext.com and search keywords:

NH SONG

NEW HAMPSHIRE TIMELINE

1600

About 5,000 members of the Abenaki and Pennacook Confederacies are living in present-day New Hampshire when French and British explorers arrive.

1620

The Pilgrims establish a colony in the New World in present-day Massachusetts.

1623

British colonists found New Hampshire's first permanent settlements at present-day Rye and Dover.

1641

The first New Hampshire colonies unite under Massachusetts' rule.

1679 King Charles II divides New Hampshire and Massachusetts into separate colonies.

1775–1783 American colonists fight for their independence from Great Britain in the Revolutionary War.

1788 New Hampshire becomes the 9th U.S. state on June 21.

1809 New Hampshire's first cotton mill is built on Amoskeag Falls near Manchester.

 **1861–1865**

The Union and the Confederacy fight the Civil War. New Hampshire fights on the Union side.

1914–1918

World War I is fought; the United States enters the war in 1917.

1929

Sig Buchmayr opens the first American ski school on Sugar Hill.

1939–1945

World War II is fought; the United States enters the war in 1941.

1961 Alan B. Shepard Jr., of East Derry, becomes the first American to travel in space.

 **1964** New Hampshire becomes the first state to hold a lottery to provide financial support to its school system.

 **1986** New Hampshire teacher Christa McAuliffe is killed when the space shuttle *Challenger* explodes.

 **1996** Jeanne Shaheen is the first woman elected governor of New Hampshire.

2007 New Hampshire becomes the first U.S. state to recognize same-sex unions.

2008 Ice storms damage the state's electrical grids. A state of emergency is declared.

2013 Thirteen towns celebrate their 250th anniversary. They are Lancaster, Lisbon, Haverhill, Warren, Woodstock, Thornton, Sandwich, Plymouth, Croydon, Alstead, Gilsum, New Boston, and Candia.

2015 *Guinness World Records* recognizes the longest pinewood derby track in the world at the New Hampshire Motor Speedway.

Glossary

abundant *(uh-BUN-duhnt)*—having plenty of something

executive *(ig-ZE-kyuh-tiv)*—the branch of government that makes sure laws are followed

industry *(IN-duh-stree)*—a business which produces a product or provides a service

geography *(jee-OG-ruh-fee)*—the study of the earth's physical features

greenhouse *(GREEN-houss)*—a warm building where plants can grow

legislature *(LEJ-iss-lay-chur)*—a group of elected officials who have the power to make or change laws for a country or state

lottery *(LOT-ur-ee)*—a way of raising money in which people buy tickets with the aim of winning a prize

natural resource *(NACH-ur-uhl REE-sorss)*—something in nature that people use, such as coal and trees

province *(PROV-uhnss)*—a district or a region of some countries

textile *(TEK-stile)*—a fabric or cloth that has been woven or knitted

tourism *(TOOR-i-zuhm)*—the business of taking care of visitors to a country or place

Read More

Ganeri, Anita. *United States of America: A Benjamin Blog and His Inquisitive Dog Guide.* Country Guides. Chicago: Heinemann Raintree, 2015.

Rissman, Rebecca. *What's Great About New Hampshire?* Our Great States. Minneapolis: Lerner Publications, 2015.

Waring, Kerry Jones. *New Hampshire: The Granite State.* It's My State! New York: Cavendish Square Publishing, 2016.

Internet Sites

FactHound offers a safe, fun way to find Internet sites related to this book. All of the sites on FactHound have been researched by our staff.

Here's all you do:

Visit *www.facthound.com*

Type in this code: 9781515704164

 Check out projects, games and lots more at
www.capstonekids.com

Critical Thinking Using the Common Core

1. What are New Hampshire's five largest cities? (Key Ideas and Details)

2. In 1964 New Hampshire became the first state to hold a lottery to provide financial support to its school system. What is a lottery? (Craft and Structure)

3. America's Stonehenge is named after a group of similar stone monuments in England. What was the purpose of these stones? (Key Ideas and Details)

Index